THE HEALTHY HAPPY BRAIN

Engage Your Brain with Puzzles, Mazes, Word Searches, and More!

MARY EAKIN

HARVEST HOUSE PUBLISHERS
EUGENE, OREGON

To my kids, Tristan and Mia, with love.

Cover and Interior design by Mary Eakin

Happy, Healthy Brain
Copyright © 2019 by Mary Eakin
www.maryeakin.com

Published by Harvest House Publishers
Eugene, Oregon 97408
www.harvesthousepublishers.com

Some material previously published by Harvest House Publishers in *Mind Delights* and *Brain Snacks* by Mary Eakin.

ISBN 978-0-7369-7763-0 (pbk)

Printed in the United States of America

19 20 21 22 23 24 25 26 27 / VP / 10 9 8 7 6 5 4 3 2 1

Do Something Nice for Your Brain Today

Do you ever feel guilty taking a few minutes out of your busy schedule just to relax?

Could you use an encouraging word to balance out the cares of your day?

Are you ready for a fun way to refresh your heart and renew your mind?

Here's your invitation to enjoy a few quiet moments resetting your focus while gently stimulating your brain. These entertaining and beautifully illustrated activities are specially designed to sharpen your powers of observation, bolster your problem-solving skills, and spur your creativity. At the same time, the Scripture verses and hope-filled thoughts will lighten your spirit and help you maintain a positive outlook throughout your day.

Your brain works hard all day long. Here's your chance to make it a little happier and healthier. Have fun!

"[He brings forth] food from the earth
and wine that makes glad the heart of
man, oil to make his face shine,
and bread which strengthens
man's heart."

PSALM 104:14-15 NKJV

CIRCLE 7 DIFFERENCES you can find
on this picture.

TEST YOUR MEMORY!

Look at the previous two pages for one minute and see how many questions you can answer below.

1. How many bunches of grapes are there?

....

2. "And bread which strenghtens a man's..." What does it strengthen?

....

3. How many glasses are there?

....

4. One of the differences is a missing grape. True or false?

....

5. Is the Bible verse from Matthew or the Psalms?

....

6. There are one, two, or three types of fruit shown?

....

7. There is cheese on the plate. True or false?

....

CHALLENGE YOURSELF!

*Fill in each row, each column, and each 9-box square
with the numbers 1 through 9.*

when it's raining

It's a gift from above.

SPICE OF LIFE

Solve the puzzle on these spicy words.

DOWN

1. Sweet, licorice-like
2. "Please pass the _____ and pepper!"
3. Used in coleslaw and potato salad
4. Purpleish color, tart flavor
5. Tangy, earthy taste

ACROSS

6. One of the oldest oilseed crops known
7. Popular in Middle Eastern dishes
8. A member of the parsley family
9. Common in Mexican cooking
10. Flowering plant in the carrot family
11. Strong breath

A good rest makes a

2•   3•   13• 14• 21• 29•   35•   36•38 39• 45•   46•   52• •53
15

4•

    16   22   44• 43•
6• 5•7 18 17 23 24   42   47• 51•
28• 30 •34
8•   27• 31 •33   48• 50•
9• 19   49•
1•11 •10 12 20 25 26•32 37 40• 41• 54• 55•

morning.

REVEAL some of nature's beauty.

For help on how to complete nonograms, see the end of this book.

The best kind
of people
are

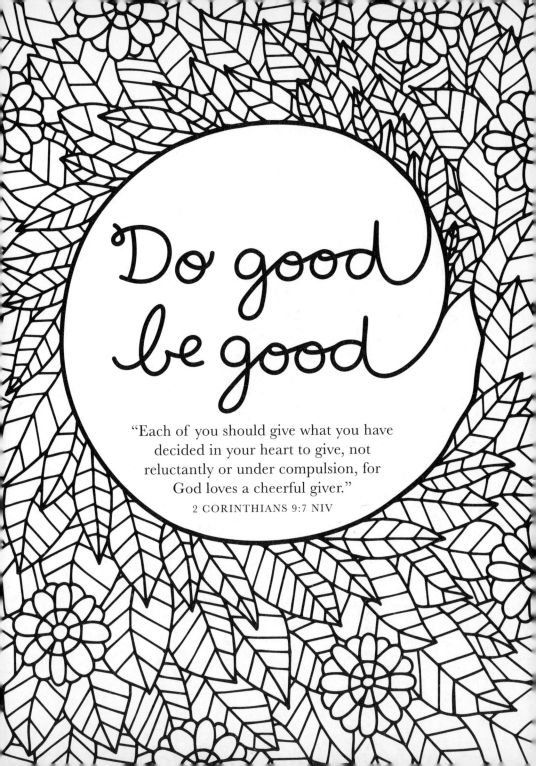

Do good
be good

"Each of you should give what you have decided in your heart to give, not reluctantly or under compulsion, for God loves a cheerful giver."

2 CORINTHIANS 9:7 NIV

"Now there are diversities of gifts, but the same Spirit. And there are differences of administrations, but the same Lord."

1 CORINTHIANS 12:4-5 KJV

CIRCLE 7 DIFFERENCES you can find on this picture.

TEST YOUR MEMORY!

Look at the previous two pages for one minute and see how many questions you can answer below.

1. How many flowers are there?

....

2. "Now there are diversities of gifts, but the same..." what?

....

3. Is the bird's eye open or closed?

....

4. There is a bee on one of the flowers. True or false?

....

5. How many tail feathers are there?

....

6. Are the bird's feet shown?

....

7. One of the differences is a missing flower. True or false?

....

DRAW your favorite food.

FIND THE WORDS that could give joy to the world.

"The Son of Man came not to be served but to serve others
and to give his life as a ransom for many."

MARK 10:45 NLT

FEEDING, HEALING, HELPING, VOLUNTEERING, SERVING,
RECYCLING, CAREGIVING, TEACHING, SMILING, COMFORTING

```
U N T G V O L U N T N E R I N G
T R O F M O G N I T R O F M O C
N I T R O F N G N I H C N F G A
N E G A G N I H C A E T G V N R
O G N H N O L O E S E I N I G E
A I I E R M C M I R M A I N H G
O V P A O L Y C N F G I P L O I
C N F L E M C R O F M O L E F V
E E D I F E E D I N G P E I N I
E S G N I V R E S V N V H E N N
U N T G V O L U N T E E R I N G
```

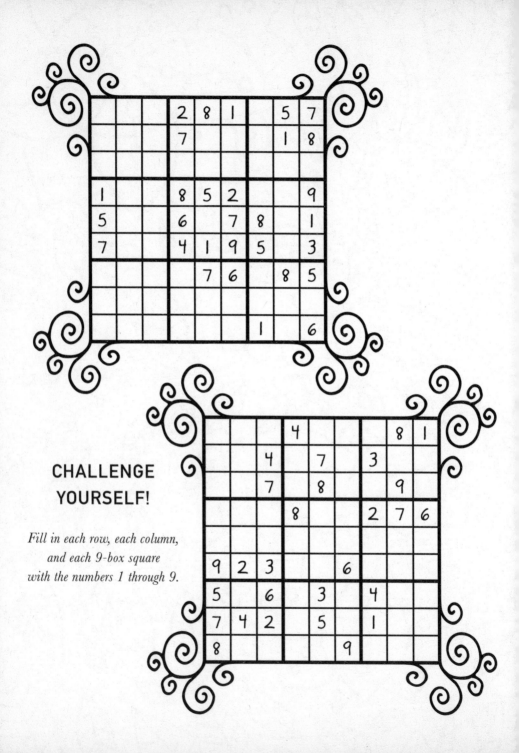

CHALLENGE YOURSELF!

Fill in each row, each column, and each 9-box square with the numbers 1 through 9.

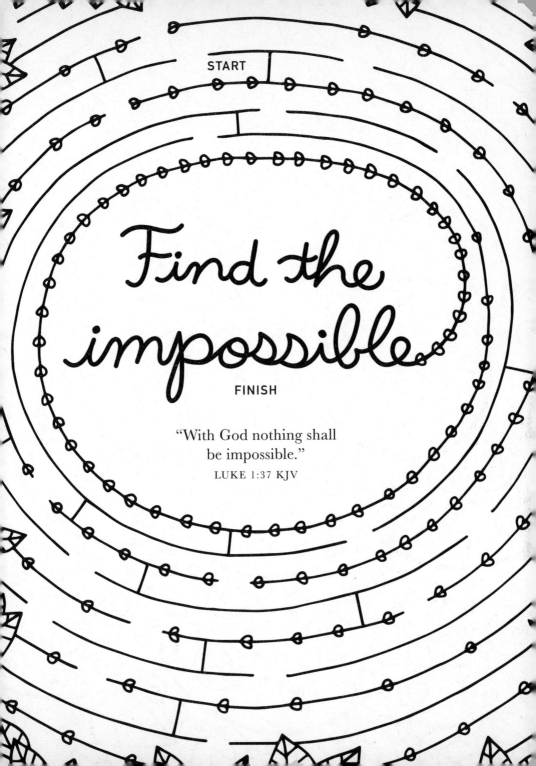

START

Find the impossible

FINISH

"With God nothing shall
be impossible."
LUKE 1:37 KJV

Find the words that help you achieve a goal.

```
O V R       B E
C I F W B E S P E C I F I C
A O M R O T S N I A R B I A
S E N V I S I O N S U C C E S S
I O T S T A Y M O T I V A T E D
T M G I E N I L E M I T A T E S
D E C I D E O N A G O A L O V
S T S T I H T I W K C I T S
H A D M A K E A P L A N
E I O A K E A O
L E W D O
P I N
```

DECIDE ON A GOAL,
SET A TIMELINE, MAKE A PLAN,
WRITE IT DOWN, BE SPECIFIC,
BRAINSTORM, STICK WITH IT, GET HELP,
STAY MOTIVATED, ENVISION SUCCESS

Good food
+
(Good friends)
=

1   3   2   16   23   25

              15 •   •17

              •14   18 •   24 • 22

       4

8   13   19
   7   5
9   6   11   20
   10   12   21

REVEAL some of nature's beauty.

For help on how to complete nonograms, see the end of this book.

"Give her of the fruit of her hands,
and let her works praise her in the gates."

PROVERBS 31:31 ESV

CIRCLE 7 DIFFERENCES you can find on this picture.

DRAW your favorite hobby.

CHALLENGE YOURSELF!

Fill in each row, each column, and each 9-box square
with the numbers 1 through 9.

Puzzle 1

9	6			8				
						3	6	
			7		1		5	
			6	9			7	
3		1	7					
	6		5				2	
							1	
		9	5			4		
	3	4	8					

Puzzle 2

		3	4				2	
8				2				9
	5		9		6			
1								
	8	6	3		5	2	7	
								6
		5		2		8		
3			9					1
	6				8	9		

"The entire law is fulfilled in keeping
this one command: 'Love your neighbor
as yourself.'"

GALATIANS 5:14 NIV

CIRCLE 7 DIFFERENCES you can find
on this picture.

TEST YOUR MEMORY!

Look at the previous two pages for one minute and see how many questions you can answer below.

1. How many flowers and birds are there?

....

2. Where are the birds looking?

....

3. How many leaves are on the middle flower?

....

4. One of the birds is sitting. True or false?

....

5. What book of the Bible is the quote from?

....

6. Are the birds surrounded by floating leaves, circles, or both?

....

7. How many differences are in the picture?

....

DRAW something you admire.

"You have turned my mourning into joyful dancing. You have taken away my clothes of mourning and clothed me with joy."

PSALM 30:11 NLT

**CIRCLE 7
DIFFERENCES**
you can find
on this picture.

TEST YOUR MEMORY!

Look at the previous two pages for one minute and see how many questions you can answer below.

1. What type of bird is there?

....

2. How many birds are there?

....

3. Complete this sentence: "You have turned my mourning into joyful..." what?

....

4. The birds' eyes are open. True or false?

....

5. What version of the Bible is the quote from?

....

6. How many trees are there?

....

7. Is the Bible quote to the right or left of the bird?

....

REVEAL some of nature's beauty.

For help on how to complete nonograms, see the end of this book.

Column clues (left to right, read top to bottom):

2	4					8	9	9	12						12	9	9	8					4	2
2	4	12	13	13	12	3	3	2	3	12	11	7	7	11	3	2	3	3	12	13	13	12	4	2
2	2	2	2	2	2	2	2	2	3	16	2	2	2	16	3	2	2	2	2	2	2	2	2	2

Row clues (top to bottom):

		4	4
			11
	3	13	3
			23
			25
			25
			23
		11	9
		11	10
8	3	2	8
6	3	2	6
7	2	1	7
		6	6
		8	8
3	3	3	3
		2	2
		1	1
		1	1
		1	1
		1	1
		1	1
		1	1
		1	1
		1	1
		1	1
		1	1
		1	1
		2	2
			25
			25

FOLLOW the good path.

"Listen, my son, and be wise, and set your heart on the right path."

PROVERBS 23:19 NIV

Improve

"Behold, happy is the man whom God corrects; therefore do not despise the chastening of the Almighty."

JOB 5:17 NKJV

CHALLENGE YOURSELF!

Fill in each row, each column, and each 9-box square
with the numbers 1 through 9.

DRAW a thing or a place you want to see.

EXPLORE YOUR WORLD

Solve the puzzle on these fabulous locales.

DOWN

1. City-state and island
2. Petronas Towers
3. Capital of South Korea
4. Stands on the river Thames
5. Crossing point of Asia and Europe

ACROSS

6. The most skyscrapers
7. Origin around a dam
8. Largest city in Czech Republic
9. 2016 Summmber Olympics
10. Battle of York site
11. Capital of Hungary
12. Means "sheltered harbor"

"He has told you,
O man, what is good;
and what does the LORD
require of you but to do
justice, and to love kindness,
and to walk humbly with
your God?"

MICAH 6:8 ESV

FIND THE WORDS that make people smile.

"God has made laughter for me;
everyone who hears will laugh with me."
GENESIS 21:6 NASB

O L S N B A L L O O N S O L S
S U S E C S E I P P U P S
S N N S N O W A N G E L S G S E
I P F R P W F P S H P H P H S H S
S M C I S M F U M U S I C I M C U
S C S O C E A N G A N E E G
E W E E K E N D S K D S W K D S
S O C E A S I C I M C E O N D S N

COFFEE

BALLOONS

SNOW ANGELS

WEEKENDS

SUNRISE

OCEAN

HUGS

MUSIC

PIE

PUPPIES

"Be strong and do not let your hands be weak, for your
work shall be rewarded!"

2 CHRONICLES 15:7 NKJV

CIRCLE 7 DIFFERENCES you can find
on this picture.

"I shall give you rains
in their season, so that the land
will yield its produce and
the trees of the field will bear
their fruit."

LEVITICUS 26:4 NASB

FIND THE WORDS that increase opportunity.

VOLUNTEER, GET OUTSIDE, EDUCATION, BEST EFFORT,
SOCIALIZE, READ, TRY NEW THINGS, KEEP STRIVING,
MAKE MISTAKES, BE KIND

REVEAL some of nature's beauty.

For help on how to complete nonograms, see the end of this book.

Column clues (top, read top to bottom):

6	7	8			4		2		2		4			8	7	6								
4	3	2		5		3	2	6	1		1	6	2	3		5		2	3	4				
11	2	1	1	4	3		3	2	1	5	3	5	3	5	1	2	3		3	4	1	1	2	11
2	3	3	2	15	4	8	3	2	1	2	1	3	1	2	1	2	3	8	4	15	2	3	3	2
10	6	7	8	4	5	8	3	4	6	5	2	5	2	5	6	4	3	8	5	4	8	7	6	10

Row clues (left, read left to right):

- 25
- 25
- 11 1 11
- 7 3 1 3 7
- 4 3 7 3 4
- 5 4 4 5
- 1 7 7 1
- 2 4 4 2
- 3 2 2 3
- 5 5
- 5 5
- 1 2 2 1
- 5 1 1 5
- 2 1 1 2
- 3 7 3
- 6 5 6
- 3 2 3 2 3
- 2 4 4 2
- 1 7 7 1
- 5 4 4 5
- 4 3 7 3 4
- 7 3 1 3 7
- 11 1 11
- 25
- 25

2• 3• 12• 14 13• 20• 23• 26• 28 27• •35 37• 39• 38•

4•

6• 5•7 17 16• 31 29• 30• 42 40• 41•
15• 15•

8•

1• 9• 11• 19• 22• 25• 34• 44•
10 18 21 24 32 33 36 43

in yourself

"The way of a fool is right in his own eyes,
but he who heeds counsel is wise."

PROVERBS 12:15 NKJV

DRAW someone completly relaxed.

"What we suffer now is nothing
compared to the glory he will reveal
to us later."

ROMANS 8:18 NLT

CIRCLE 7 DIFFERENCES
you can find
on this picture.

FIND a way to get

inspired

FINISH

START

FIND THE WORDS that make a happy home.

```
E J E V H Y L A U G T H E R S G E
D O O F D O O G P E A C E S N S E
R N G U S T D N S T C N S R O G S
E L P N U R S I R D A P D A I U D
A J O Y M D R R S T W A R M T H R
M R S V H Y L A U G H T E R I R E
S T D C E T D C F A M I L Y D E L
T Y A S M D V A V S A E Y S A S Y
R W E L C O M E S I G N A A R T A
S T O V H T N R E S A C R S T F R
T Y A S E R O A V O G E E R S U E
T Y A S M D V A V S A E Y S O L Y
```

LOVE, WARMTH, LAUGHTER, CARING, DREAMS,
GOOD FOOD, HUGS, PATIENCE, FUN,
FAMILY, TRADITIONS, WELCOME SIGN, HAVEN,
RESTFUL, PEACE, JOY

Take care of

There's only one.

1   3   15   19 23   33 35   49 50
    9   37 36 43
                  24   32 34
      8   10   31
2 4   26 25   38 39   48 47
                  30 40   46
7   11 16 20   29
    14 18
5   6   13 21   42   45
    12 17 22   27   28   41 44

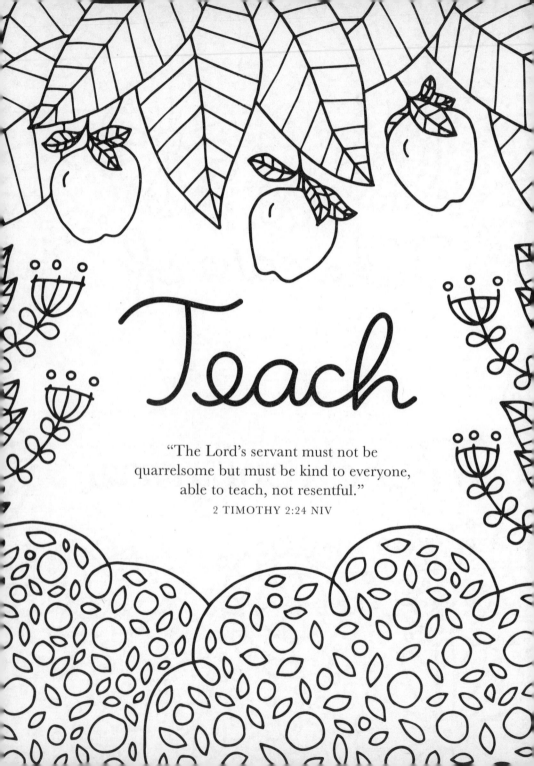

Teach

"The Lord's servant must not be quarrelsome but must be kind to everyone, able to teach, not resentful."

2 TIMOTHY 2:24 NIV

REVEAL some of nature's beauty.

For help on how to complete nonograms, see the end of this book.

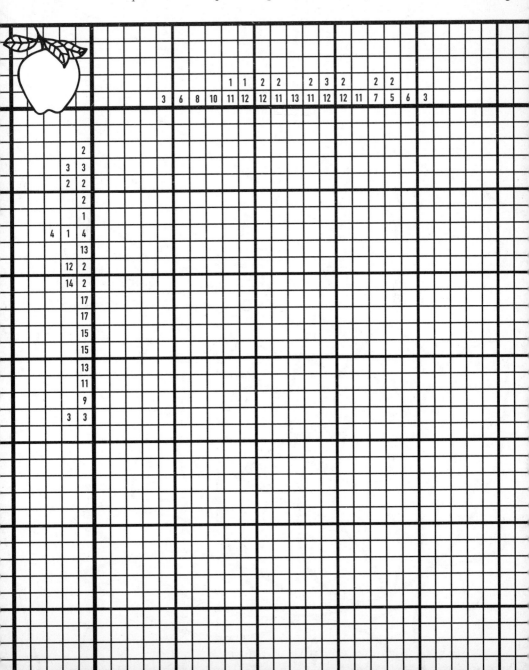

"Your word is a lamp to my feet
and a light to my path."
PSALM 119:105 NASB

CIRCLE 7 DIFFERENCES
you can find
on this picture.

Illuminate

"God saw that the light was good; and God separated the light from the darkness."

GENESIS 1:4 NASB

DRAW something illuminated.

FOLLOW the path you choose.

1
2
3
4

On the umbrella, **DRAW** your favorite thing to do when it's raining.

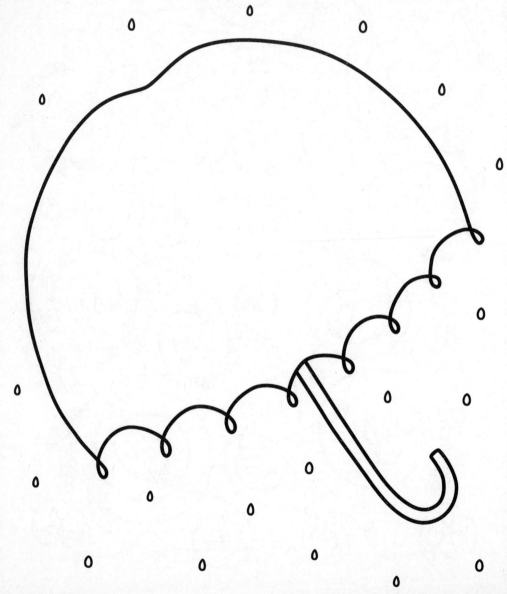

"The LORD is my light and my salvation—
so why should I be afraid?
The LORD is my fortress, protecting
me from danger,
so why should I tremble?"

PSALM 27:1 NLT

CIRCLE 7 DIFFERENCES
you can find
on this picture.

TEST YOUR MEMORY!

Look at the previous two pages for one minute and see how many questions you can answer below.

1. How many insects are there?

....

2. "The LORD is my light and my..." what?

....

3. What psalm is the Bible quote from?

....

4. One of the differences is a missing heart. True or false?

....

5. Does the upper-right corner have leaves or rain?

....

6. How many circles are on each insect?

....

7. All the flowers have circles on them. True or false?

....

FOR THE BIRDS

Solve the puzzle about these beautiful winged creatures.

DOWN

1. Noisy little bird
2. Flaps wings very fast
3. Metaphor in Charles Baudelaine poem
4. Giving thanks
5. Who?
6. Peace

ACROSS

7. Scavenger
8. Likes to repeat
9. Short and wide beak with long eyes
10. Waddles about

DRAW something that exists only in your imagination.

"Love is patient, love is kind and is not jealous;
love does not brag and is not arrogant, does not act
unbecomingly; it does not seek its own, is not provoked,
does not take into account a wrong suffered."

1 CORINTHIANS 13:4-5 NASB

CIRCLE 7 DIFFERENCES you can find on this picture.

TEST YOUR MEMORY!

Look at the previous two pages for one minute and see how many
questions you can answer below.

1. How many acorns are there?

....

2. "Love is patient, love is kind and is not..." what?

....

3. What chapter of 1 Corinthians is the Bible quote from?

....

4. The squirrels are frowning. True or false?

....

5. Are the acorns in the middle of the page or to the side of the squirrels?

....

6. Are the squirrels' eyes open or closed?

....

7. There are no circles on the acorns. True or false?

....

REVEAL some of nature's beauty.

For help on how to complete nonograms, see the end of this book.

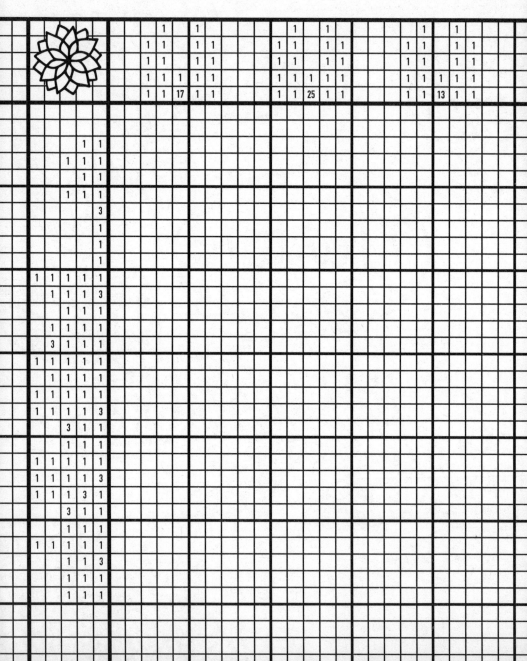

It's going to be

EVERY DAY

CHALLENGE YOURSELF!

*Fill in each row, each column, and each 9-box square
with the numbers 1 through 9.*

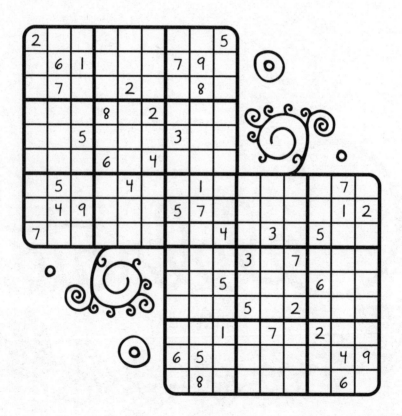

Soar

"The wild animals honor me,
the jackals and the owls, because
I provide water in the wilderness and
streams in the wasteland, to give
drink to my people, my chosen."

ISAIAH 43:20 NIV

"Arise, shine, for your light has come,
and the glory of the LORD rises upon you."

ISAIAH 60:1 NIV

CIRCLE 7 DIFFERENCES you can find
on this picture.

DRAW yourself overcoming an obstacle you face.

REVEAL some of nature's beauty.

For help on how to complete nonograms, see the end of this book.

Column clues (top to bottom):

								3		3	2		2	3		3								
			3	2	1			1	3	1	1		1	1	3	1			1	2	3			
		5	2	1	1	2	2	1	3	1	1		1	1	3	1	2	2	1	1	2	5		
5	7	4	3	3	2	2	1	2	2	3	2	2	2	3	2	2	1	2	2	3	3	4	7	5
4	6	3	4	5	6	6	5	4	3	2	1	9	1	2	3	4	5	6	6	5	4	3	6	4

Row clues (top to bottom):

- 5
- 7
- 3 3 3 3
- 6 2 2 6
- 4 3 3 4
- 3 1 1 3
- 3 1 1 3
- 2 2
- 2 1 1 2
- 3 1 1 3
- 4 1 1 4
- 2 1 1 2
- 3 1 1 3
- 2 1 1 2
- 2 1 1 2
- 3 3
- 3 3
- 3 1 1 3
- 5 5
- 3 1 1 3
- 3 3
- 1 7 1
- 2 5 2
- 3 1 3
- 4 1 4
- 4 1 4
- 5 1 5
- 5 1 5
- 6 1 6
- 13

Time to

DRAW yourself truly happy

"Getting wisdom is the wisest thing you can do!
And whatever else you do, develop good judgment."
PROVERBS 4:7 NLT

CIRCLE 7 DIFFERENCES you can find
on this picture.

TEST YOUR MEMORY!

Look at the previous two pages for one minute and see how many questions you can answer below.

1. How many insects are there?

....

2. "Whatever else you do, develop..." what?

....

3. Are the foxes laying down or sitting?

....

4. One fox has an eye open. True or false?

....

5. Name three of the differences between the two pages.

....

6. How many circles are on the foxes?

....

7. The Bible quote is from Proverbs. True or false?

....

"Save yourself like a gazelle escaping
from a hunter,
like a bird fleeing from a net."

PROVERBS 6:5 NLT

Elevate

CHALLENGE YOURSELF!

*Fill in each row, each column, and each 9-box square
with the numbers 1 through 9.*

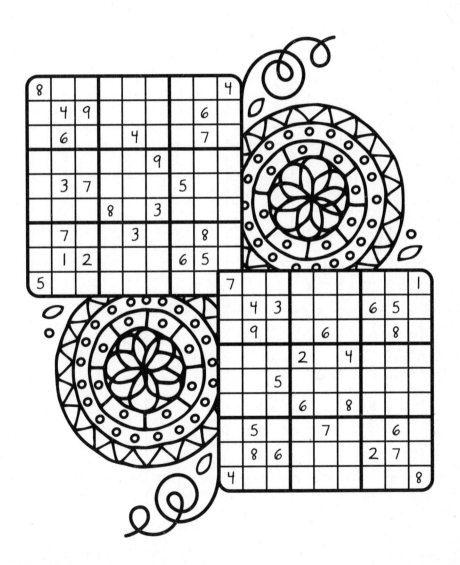

Column clues (top):

																		3	2				
4	2	1	2	4	5	6				12		4	9	8	3	4							
6	5	11	9	8	7	9	11	13	12	11	10	11	10	24	16	4	4	6	6	14	16	17	
30	21	20	5	4	3	3	3	4	5	15	14	14	14	2	1	1	1	2	8	8	8	9	10	30

Row clues (left):

		25
	5	19
4	11	6
4	10	5
3	8	4
2	7	4
1	6	4
1	7	5
	1	15
	2	16
3	4	12
4	4	11
	10	10
10	5	4
10	4	3
11	5	3
	18	2
	17	1
	17	1
6	10	1
5	10	2
4	10	3
	3	15
3	6	8
3	5	7
4	5	6
5	6	6
	14	6
	15	7
		25

DRAW something you have marveled at.

"See that none render evil for evil unto any man; but ever follow that which is good, both among yourselves, and to all men."

1 THESSALONIANS 5:15 KJV

CIRCLE 7 DIFFERENCES you can find
on this picture.

TEST YOUR MEMORY!

Look at the previous two pages for one minute and see how many questions you can answer below.

1. How many birds are there?

....

2. "See that none render evil for..." what?

....

3. How many full circles did you see on the small owl's head?

....

4. One of the differences is a swirl. True or false?

....

5. Is the Bible version KJV or NIV?

....

6. How many wings are shown?

....

7. There are stripes in one of the circles. True or false?

....

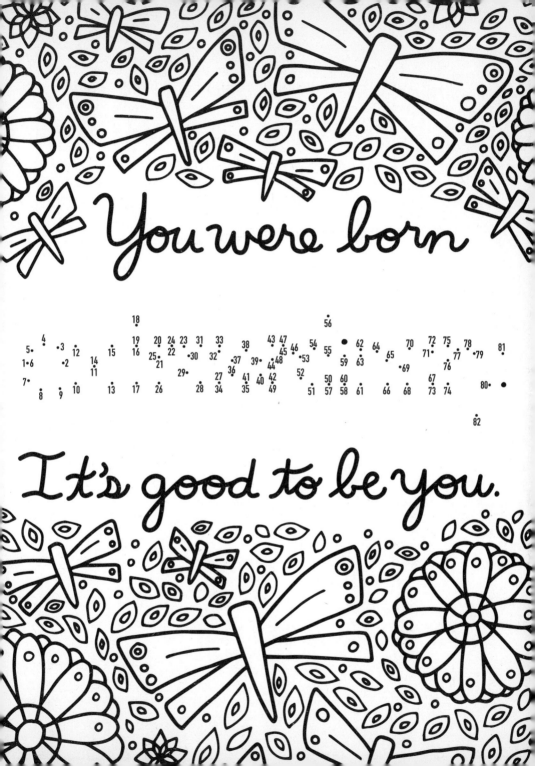

DRAW what would make you happy right now.

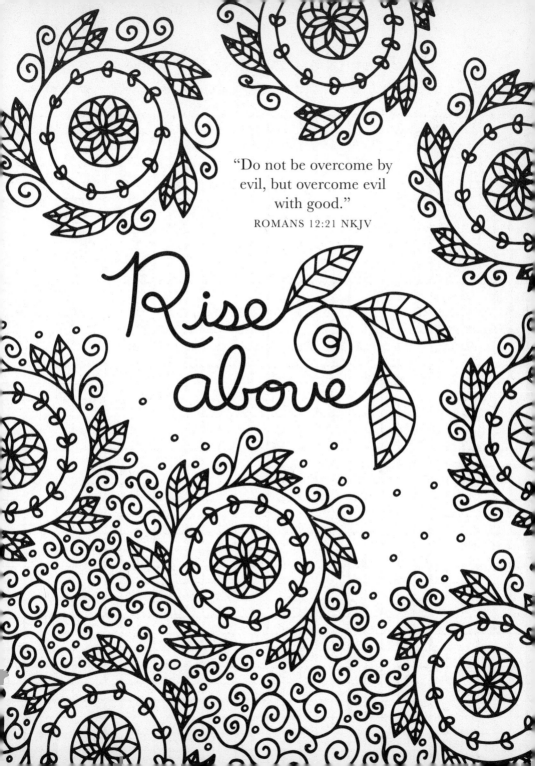

"Do not be overcome by evil, but overcome evil with good."

ROMANS 12:21 NKJV

Rise above

REVEAL some of nature's beauty.

For help on how to complete nonograms, see the end of this book.

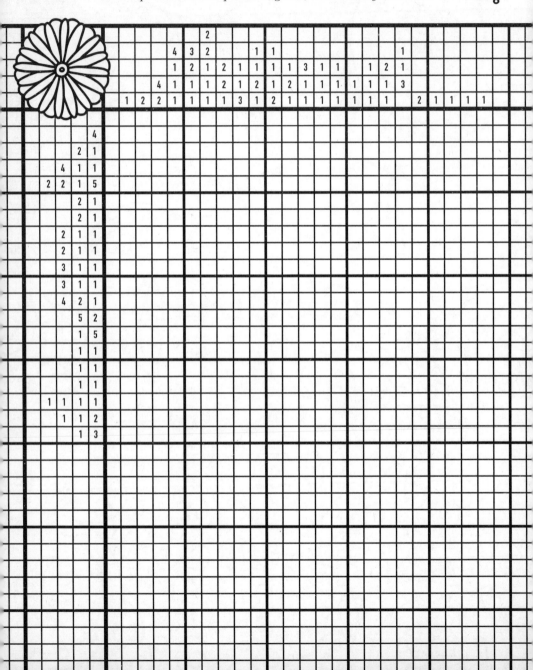

Delight

"This is the day the LORD has made. We will rejoice and be glad in it."

PSALM 118:24 NLT

"Let love be without hypocrisy. Abhor what is evil.
Cling to what is good."

ROMANS 12:9 NKJV

CIRCLE 7 DIFFERENCES you can find
on this picture.

TEST YOUR MEMORY!

Look at the previous two pages for one minute and see how many questions you can answer below.

1. How many flowers are there?

....

2. "Let love be without..." what?

....

3. Do the flowers have one, two, or three circles?

....

4. One of the differences is on a deer's eye. True or false?

....

5. Is the Bible version KJV, NIV, or something else?

....

6. How many deer hooves are shown?

....

7. There is a small insect in the picture. True or false?

....

wish

"If you remain in me and my words remain in you, ask whatever you wish, and it will be done for you."

JOHN 15:7 NIV

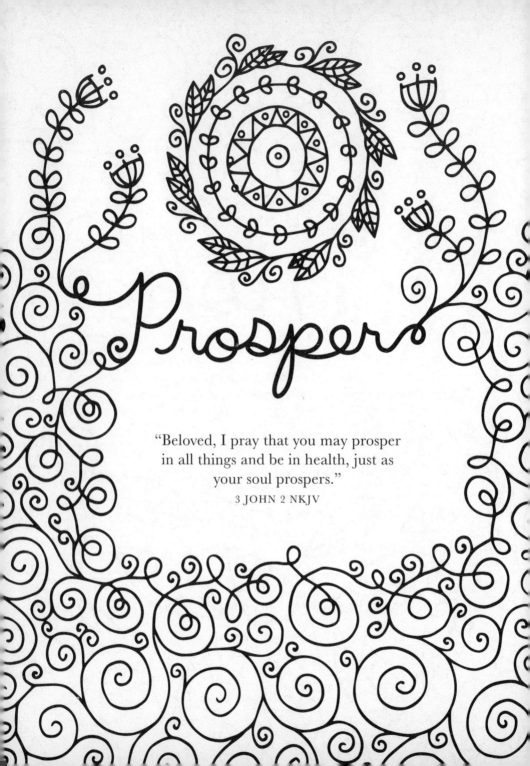

Prosper

"Beloved, I pray that you may prosper
in all things and be in health, just as
your soul prospers."

3 JOHN 2 NKJV

DRAW what it means to prosper.

START

Find a way to happy

FINISH

"I know that there is nothing better for people than to be happy and to do good while they live."

ECCLESIASTES 3:12-13 NIV

CHALLENGE YOURSELF!

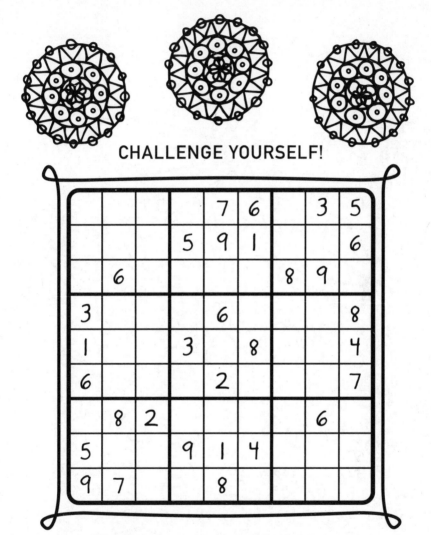

				7	6		3	5
			5	9	1			6
	6					8	9	
3				6				8
1			3		8			4
6				2				7
	8	2					6	
5			9	1	4			
9	7			8				

*Fill in each row, each column, and each 9-box square
with the numbers 1 through 9.*

"Ask, and it shall be given you; seek, and ye shall find; knock, and it shall be opened unto you."

MATTHEW 7:7 KJV

CIRCLE 7 DIFFERENCES you can find on this picture.

TEST YOUR MEMORY!

Look at the previous two pages for one minute and see how many questions you can answer below.

1. How many insects are there?

....

2. "...and it shall be given unto you." What do you have to do?

....

3. How many flowers are there?

....

4. One of the differences is a missing insect. True or false?

....

5. Is the Bible verse from Matthew or Proverbs?

....

6. Do the insects have more than three stripes or fewer?

....

7. There are eight differences on the right page. True or false?

....

STOP AND SMELL THE FLOWERS

Solve the puzzle on these calming flora.

DOWN

1. Named after French botanist Pierre _____
2. The common name is rocktrumpet
3. From Greek meaning "water vessel"
4. Of the genus *Campanula*
5. One of the first shrubs to bloom in spring

ACROSS

6. Sometimes called mums
7. Originating from Argentina and Chile
8. The other red holiday flower
9. Can be a sign of eternal love, prophetic dreams, healing, or wealth
10. Thirtieth anniversary flower
11. In the rose family

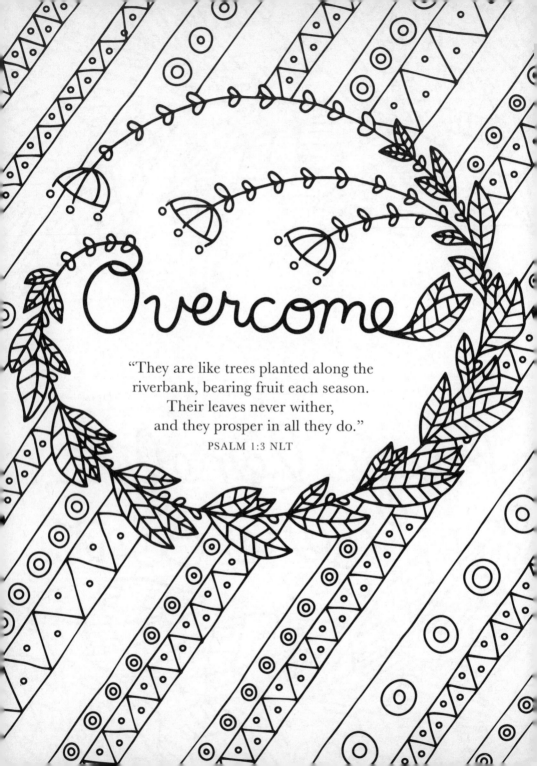

Overcome

"They are like trees planted along the riverbank, bearing fruit each season. Their leaves never wither, and they prosper in all they do."

PSALM 1:3 NLT

DRAW someone overcoming a difficulty.

"Let your light so shine before men, that they may see your good works, and glorify your Father which is in heaven."

MATTHEW 5:16 KJV

CIRCLE 7
DIFFERENCES
you can find
on this picture.

TEST YOUR MEMORY!

Look at the previous two pages for one minute and see how many questions you can answer below.

1. How many birds are there?

....

2. "Let your light so shine before men, that they may see your..." what?

....

3. What is the shape around the words?

....

4. One of the differences is a worm. True or false?

....

5. Was the Bible verse from Matthew or Psalms?

....

6. Are the birds' eyes open or closed?

....

7. One difference is a spot on the beak. True or false?

....

FIND THE WORDS that make
a happy table.

```
C P A S T R I E S T
O A S T R T A R T S
P B I E S T I E C R O R
S B P S B E R W A E N E
K O L P U R S T R K U N R G
S T E O C O O K I E S I C N
S T R R N O W C P A S E O S I N
A S T R I C N A S T R L T A D T
M A E R C E C I U O K I E E S D O S
N R K L C A K E P O P S K E I U S P
D O U G H N U T S E L C I S P O P N S E
```

ICE CREAM, PASTRIES, DOUGHNUTS, POPSICLES, PUDDING, CAKE,
TARTS, COBBLER, STREUSEL, BROWNIES, CAKE POPS, COOKIES, PIE

DRAW something that grows.

"I am with
you always."
MATTHEW 28:20 KJV

CIRCLE 7
DIFFERENCES
you can find on
this picture.

TEST YOUR MEMORY!

Look at the previous two pages for one minute and see how many questions you can answer below.

1. How many leaves are there?

....

2. Finish the sentence. "I am..."

....

3. Are there any insects?

....

4. One of the differences is an extra leaf. True or false?

....

5. Is the Bible verse from Genesis or Matthew?

....

6. Is the Bible version KJV or NIV?

....

7. There are more than 60 circles on the two pages. True or false?

....

Take a walk

"Arise, walk about the land through its
length and breadth; for I will
give it to you."
GENESIS 13:17 NASB

FIND a happy heart.

FINISH

START

"A cheerful heart is good medicine, but a broken spirit saps a person's strength."

PROVERBS 17:22 NLT

DRAW anything you like here.

"The grass withers, the flower fades,
But the word of our God stands forever."

ISAIAH 40:8 NASB

CIRCLE 7 DIFFERENCES

you can find on this picture.

TEST YOUR MEMORY!

Look at the previous two pages for one minute and see how many questions you can answer below.

1. Does the grass wither or fade?

....

2. What stands forever?

....

3. How many flowers are on the two pages?

....

4. One of the flowers has a stem. True or false?

....

5. Is the Bible verse from Genesis or Isaiah?

....

6. Is the Bible version NASB or NIV?

....

7. One of the differences is on a leaf. True or false?

....

FIND THE WORDS
to get back to nature.

```
R G R A S S G E E R F R
S N A R J U M P I N G S
D I D F L O W E R S N J
R N F P D M F J N G R L
I N N T H G I L N U S D
B U T T E R F L I E S H
G R I A H S E R F G R E
```

BUTTERFLIES, UNPLUG, FREE,
SUNLIGHT, RUNNING,
BIRDS, FRESH AIR, GRASS,
JUMPING, FLOWERS

"The Lord your God is bringing
you into a good land of flowing
streams and pools of water."
DEUTERONOMY 8:7 NLT

HOW TO SOLVE NONOGRAMS

A nonogram is a logic puzzle that, when solved, reveals something. There are many ways to solve nonograms, but here are a few tips to get you started.

• The numbers on the top and left are your clues. They tell you how many boxes in a column or row need to be colored in. Place the blocks of numbers from top to bottom and left to right.

• The number blocks cannot touch each other. There could be one or several boxes between each number clue.

• Fill in first any numbers that complete a row or column. This can help give you a clue about the rest.

• Look for any overlap.

When you have a big number, wherever you put it, some of the squares will end up solid.

• Some people use a dot or x to mark the spaces they know are empty.

• The numbers may reveal an image, a pattern, or words.

• Never guess a box to be shaded in. One error can throw off the whole puzzle.

• Have fun! If you find yourself becoming frustrated, take a break. You can always come back to it when you want to challenge yourself.

• The answer keys to the nonograms and other activities in this book can be found at maryeakin.com/answers.

Column clues (top):

7 7 7

10 8 10 10 10   5 7 3 3 3 7 7   7 7 12 12 12

6 6 6 6 6 6 6 18 18 6 6 6 6 6 6 6 20 20 4 4 4 4 4 4 7 7

Row clues (completed grid):

			1	15
			1	15
			5	18
			5	18
			5	18
			5	18
			5	18
	5	2	2	3
	5	2	2	3
5	2	3	2	3
3	2	3	2	3
3	2	3	2	3
			2	2
			2	2
				23
				23

Row clues (blank puzzle grid):

			1	15
			1	15
			5	18
			5	18
			5	18
			5	18
			5	18
	5	2	2	3
	5	2	2	3
5	2	3	2	3
3	2	3	2	3
3	2	3	2	3
			2	2
			2	2
				23
				23
				23
				23
				18
				18

ABOUT THE AUTHOR

Mary Eakin is a graduate of the Academy of
Art University of San Francisco and was an
award-winning graphic designer of Hallmark
gift books for nine years. She is the author and
illustrator of *Mind Delights, Brain Snacks,* and
My Creative Year. Mary lives with her husband
and two children in Maryland.